IK SONGBIJIT AND HIS ROLE IN INDEPENDENT BOROLAND

LEFTENANT GENERAL

Dedicated to the martyrs of Bodoland Movement.

Contents

Preface

This book deals with the role of IK Songbijit in Bodoland Movement. Hope the readers will enjoy reading it.

Ik Songbijit And His Role In Independent Boroland

LEFTENANT GENERAL

CHAPTER ONE

Introduction

Ingti Kathar Songbijit is a militant leader who once led the secessionist faction of National Democratic Front of Boroland (NDFB) in North-East India.

Although he served as the leader of an organization that claims to represent Bodo people, Songbijit is not a Bodo himself. He was born in a Karbi family. He hails from the Chelaikhati village, which is located in the Biswanath Chariali sub-division of Sonitpur district, Assam. Kathar is a sub-clan (*kurjon*) of the Ingti clan, which enjoys a high status in the Karbi society; the traditional chief priests come from the Kathar *kurjon*.

CHAPTER TWO

Songbijit and his role in NDFB

As a young man, Songbijit joined National Democratic Front of Boroland, a militant group seeking secession from India, to establish a sovereign Boroland. After a section of NDFB gave up the secessionist demand and agreed to stage talks with the government, NDFB split into two factions. Songbijit remained with the anti-talks faction NDFB (ATF), which was led by NDFB's founder Ranjan Daimary.

In 2009, Songbijit was promoted to the post of "army commander" in NDFB (ATF). In early 2010s, after Ranjan Daimary was arrested, a section of his group, now called NDFB (R), agreed to engage in talks with the government. The faction opposed to the talks elected Songbijit as the "Interim President" of NDFB on 13–14 November 2012. The new faction led by Songbijit is termed as NDFB (S) by the media and the government (Songbijit himself refers to his group as simply NDFB). In 2014, NDFB (S) was believed to have around 270 cadres and was led by a 9-member "national council". Its cadres were scattered across several camps located in Nagaland and Myanmar's Sagaing Region.

In January 2014, the Assam Police included him in the list of 15 most wanted criminals and declared a cash reward of ? 1 million for information leading to his arrest. NDFB (S) was accused by the government of carrying out the May and December 2014 attacks against Muslim migrants and Adivasi Tea tribes respectively, resulting in deaths of over a hundred civilians.

CHAPTER THREE

Links with other organisations

Songbijit's faction was known to be in touch with other secessionist militant groups, including ULFA and KLO. While ULFA seeks to establish a united sovereign Assam, KLO demands a sovereign Kamtapur for Koch people. Both these proposed states have territories overlapping with the proposed sovereign Bodoland. Songbijit justified his alliances with these groups claiming that Koch and Bodo people have common ethnic roots and NDFB has more similarities than differences with ULFA. According to him, the civilians killed in NDFB attacks were either collateral damage or those involved in anti-NDFB activities.

CHAPTER FOUR

Bodo Sovereignty Issue

In a 2013 interview, Songbijit stated that he would agree to talks, if the government agrees to hold a referendum on Bodoland independence. According to him, corruption and diversity in religion, caste and community will ultimately lead to balkanization of India "into 600 pieces".

End of Songbijit's role in NDFB

In 2015, Songbijit was deposed as the NDFB President following differences between him and other top leaders.